Little Miss Muffet

Retold by Russell Punter

Illustrated by Lorena Alvarez

Little Miss Muffet
sat on a tuffet,

eating her curds
and whey.

Along came a spider,
who dropped down beside her,

and frightened Miss Muffet away.

"Help!" cried Miss Muffet.
She ran from her tuffet,
and into the woods
down below.

"Come back!" called the spider.

He rushed off to find her.

"I'm sorry for scaring you so."

The little girl sighed.

"What a bad place to hide.

Now I'm lost! I'll be stuck here all night."

Then she heard
a deep growl,

and an ear-splitting howl.

OWWWWOOOOO!

They gave poor
Miss Muffet a fright.

A big wolf jumped out.

He said with a shout,

"It's time for my dinner, my dear."

"I'll have
little girl pie!"

"Put her down!"
came a cry.

"Don't worry – Seb Spider is here."

The wolf gave
a smile.

"I do like
your style.

But what can you do against me?"

"I'll show you," said Seb.

So he spun a strong web,

and tied the bad wolf
to a tree.

Miss Muffet said...

"Seb, what a wonderful web.

Now let's go!"

So Seb showed her the way.

Now she's friends with Seb Spider.

He hangs down
beside her,

and spins
for Miss Muffet
all day.

About the rhyme

The original version of *Little Miss Muffet* was
written over two hundred years ago.
Curds are lumps of thickened milk used to make cheese.
When milk thickens into curds, it also makes
a watery liquid known as whey.

Edited by Jenny Tyler and Lesley Sims

First published in 2013 by Usborne Publishing Ltd., Usborne House, 83-85 Saffron Hill, London EC1N 8RT, England. www.usborne.com
Copyright © 2013 Usborne Publishing Ltd.